BOUNTIFUL BLOOMS

PRESERVING FLOWERS WITH COLOUR

MILNER CRAFT SERIES

BOUNTIFUL BLOOMS

PRESERVING FLOWERS WITH COLOUR

MARGARET BURCH

SALLY MILNER PUBLISHING

First published in 1993 by
Sally Milner Publishing Pty Ltd
558 Darling Street
Rozelle NSW 2039 Australia

© Margaret Burch, 1993

Design by Wing Ping Tong
Photography by Ben Wrigley
Typeset in Australia by Asset Typesetting Pty Ltd
Printed in Singapore by Kyodo Printing Co

National Library of Australia
Cataloguing-in-Publication data:

Burch, Margaret.
    Bountiful blooms.

    ISBN 1 86351 101 6.

    1. Dried flower arrangement. 2. Flowers — Drying.
    I. Title. (Series : Milner craft series).

745.92

This book is dedicated to my family.

Acknowledgements

I would like to thank my mother, who gave me my early love of flower arranging; my father, who loved our garden and helped me to train in both Sydney and London; my husband and daughters, who encouraged me, helped with the preparation of this book and, together as a family, took delight in creating our country home and garden. Finally, I thank Alastair MacCallum, who kindly assisted with the preparation of the illustrations.

CONTENTS

Introduction

Flower preservation has been practised for centuries. Possibly the earliest form of drying and preserving to be used was the air drying method. It is unclear when sand drying came into use, although evidence of sand-dried roses has recently been found in an excavated tomb belonging to an Egyptian pharaoh from around 2500 BC. In the fourteenth century an Indian lady was known to have dried roses, presumably using sand drying, and in the sixteenth century an Italian gardening book was published in Siena in which a whole chapter was devoted to describing this technique. Victorian writers described a similar method to their readers. However, the technique was never popular in England and Europe because in these moist environments the dried flowers would quickly deteriorate.

The Americans, during pre-Independence times in the eighteenth century, were also known to produce dried flower arrangements. While sand drying was known of, and is still in use today, the most popular method of preserving flowers and foliage was air drying. The problem with sand is that it isn't a desiccant, i.e., a substance that absorbs water. All that sand does is hold the flower in its exact form while the moisture gradually evaporates, and this can take a long time.

Recently, there has been a search for new and more sophisticated substances and for methods that work more rapidly. Borax can be effective, but it is still slow. In the 1960s silica gel was found to be faster and to produce superior blooms. It is now possible, using silica gel, to retain the colour, form and texture of flowers so perfectly that they appear to be almost fresh.

The last few years have seen a renewed interest in dried flowers. Fresh flowers are no longer cheap, and the idea of being able to preserve some of the lovely blooms from the garden to create wonderfully natural-looking arrangements, garlands and posies is becoming increasingly popular.

The concepts and instructions described in this book are designed to help you create attractive and interesting floral works of art, which you will be able to use for the decoration of your home, to give as gifts, or sell for profit.

REQUIREMENTS

You will find it helpful if you have a room which you can set aside to be used, in whole or part, for the purpose of this rewarding work. This will allow you to keep your containers, tools and materials in one handy location, so that everything is easy to find. Ideally, the room should have a polished or smooth floor, because this will be easier to keep clean, particularly when fragments of flowers, stems and wire-cuttings need to be swept up after each work session. It should also have adequate shelf and bench space. Avoid dusty or dirty environments such as garages, so that your flowers don't become soiled.

If you plan to pursue this craft in a serious manner, you will need a reasonably large space for hanging the flowers to dry and for storing them. This can be done in cupboards or in the ceiling space of a clean, dry garage or shed. Don't choose areas that could become damp, such as a basement.

Most of the tools and materials you will need can be obtained from florist supply companies or well-equipped florists.

CONTAINERS FOR ARRANGEMENTS

It is important to have a collection of different types of containers in a variety of useful shapes. Whether they are made from pottery, glass or basketwear, they should be simple in design. Colours should be plain, e.g., white, green, black or bronze. The container must suit both the flowers and the decor of the room in which the arrangement is to be placed.

OASIS

Dry oasis is used to keep the flowers in place in the container. It comes in bricks and round shapes, and is easy to cut to whatever size you require.

OASIS PRONG

These are small plastic pin-holders, which are placed inside the container to keep the oasis firmly in place.

OASIS FIX OR FLORAL CLAY

This is a sticky green plastic clay which is sold in strip form on a roll. It is used to attach the oasis prongs to the inside of the container. (It can also be useful when decorating candlesticks.)

PARAFILM

This is a plastic tape which is slightly elastic and sticks tightly and smoothly to itself when stretched. It is used to cover wire stems, to join wire to foliage or flowers, and to cover wires when lengthening wire stems. The tape comes in green, brown or white.

FLORAL WIRE

This is available as plain or green-coated wire and is sold by diameter (in millimetres) or gauge. The thickest wire has the lowest gauge. It is used either for making wire stems to attach to the dried flowers, or for binding work. I keep the following sizes on hand:

1.25 mm (18 gauge) for heavy stems
0.9 mm (20 gauge) for medium stems
0.7 mm (22 gauge) for medium stems
0.55 mm (24 gauge) for light stems
0.45 mm (26 gauge) for very fine wiring and
    binding work

0.35 mm (28 gauge) for very fine wiring and binding work

0.24 mm (32 gauge — comes in reels) for binding work

0.2 mm (36 gauge — comes in reels) for binding work.

ADHESIVES

Hot glue guns are almost essential. They are available in different sizes and price ranges. The glue comes in a stick form. A clear-drying craft glue is also handy for reinforcing the petal structures of some flowers.

SILICA GEL

This is a crystalline, sand-like substance which is bright blue when dry, but after absorbing moisture, turns a pale pink colour. It is used for drying flowers that require a desiccant, e.g., roses. Use 0.5-1 mm A Type 100 per cent silica gel, which is readily available in 3 kg (6 lb) containers from chemical supply companies.

ACRYLIC SEALER

You will need a clear matt sealer to seal silica-dried flowers and foliage so that any dampness in the atmosphere is kept out.

GLYCERINE

This chemical can be purchased in liquid form from a chemist or, in a large quantity, from chemical companies. It is mixed with water to preserve mature, leafy foliage.

WAX

I use melted wax from household candles to coat the back of certain silica-dried flowers to give them extra support.

SOFT ARTIST'S BRUSH

This is used to remove any silica gel crystals and dust that may remain on flower petals after silica gel drying.

AIRTIGHT CONTAINERS

These are needed for silica gel drying and for storing the flowers that have been dried by this method. Plastic boxes and tins with airtight lids are ideal.

SECATEURS AND WIRE-CUTTERS

Excellent varieties especially designed for florist work are available. Some are designed for cutting wire as well as flower and foliage stems. If they do not cut wire, you will also need a pair of wire-cutters.

FLORIST'S TAPE OR POT TAPE

This is a firm adhesive tape, sticky on one side. It binds to dry oasis and is used to keep the oasis firmly in place in the vase or basket.

SPRAY DYE

These dyes are available in easy-to-use spray cans. I use 'Design Master' colour tool dyes as they have a large variety of colours. 'Design Master' tints are also available — they aren't quite as strong in colour and give a natural effect when sprayed lightly on faded flowers.

BASIC TECHNIQUES

Many different methods of preserving flowers and foliage have been used through time, ranging from roses being sand-dried in Ancient Egypt, to the latest technique which uses freeze-dryers. All these methods have the one aim of removing moisture from flowers and foliage while they retain their original form, shape and colour.

I use four different methods for preserving flowers and foliage:

- air drying
- silica gel drying
- glycerine preserving
- pressing

Some of these methods are more successful with flowers, some work better with foliage. Because of this, a lot of flowers can't be dried with their foliage intact (i.e., with their stems and leaves in place), and so they are usually dried separately.

All these methods have variations, and it is worth experimenting to find the one that works best for you and your selection of materials.

AIR DRYING

This is a simple technique that can involve several different variations. In general it refers to flowers and foliage being dried naturally, by hanging or by standing them upright, without the help of chemicals and desiccants. Flowers that are suitable for air drying are those that do not wilt easily and have flower heads with small blossoms on short stems. Dehydration causes shrinking, so the flowers need to be small and short-stemmed so that their shape and form are not affected. Most air-dried flowers are extremely stable once completely dry and are less likely to react to moisture in the atmosphere thus sagging or losing colour. If dried quickly in a warm, dry, dark place, they should retain their colours perfectly. The colour will fade gradually, especially if exposed to strong sunlight, and eventually, usually after one year, air-dreid flowers will become discoloured by dust.

Some of the flowers and foliage that are suitable for air drying include:

acroclinium (*Acroclinium roseum*)
ammobium daisy (*Ammobium alatum*)
Argyle apple (*Eucalyptus cinerea*)
artemisia (*A. rutans*)
astilbe (*Saxifragaceae*)
baby's breath (*Gypsophila paniculata*)
bay leaves (*Laurus nobilis*)
bells of Ireland (*Mollucella laevis*)
blazing star (*Liatris spicata*)
blue salvia (*Salvia farinacea*)
celosia (*Amaranthaceae*)
Chinese lantern (*Physalis franchetii*)
chive flowers (*Allium schoenoprasum*)
cornflower (*Centaurea cyanus*)
curry flower (*Lysinema ciliatum*)
delphinium (*D. hybridum*)
erigeron (*Compositae fleabane*)
eucalyptus (*E. crenulata*) leaves
globe amaranth (*Gomphrena globosa*)
globe thistle (*Echinops ritro*)
golden rod (*Solidago canadensis*)
honesty (*Lunaria*)
hydrangea (*Saxifragaceae*)
lamb's tongue (*Stachys lanata*)
larkspur (*Delphinium ujacis*)
lavender (*Lavandula*)
leek flowers (*Allium ampeloprasum* var. *porrum*)
lonas (*L. inodora*)
love-in-a-mist (*Nigella damascena*)
love-lies-bleeding (*Amaranthus*)
poppy (*Papaver*) seed heads
pussy willow (*Salix caprea*)
Queen Anne's lace (*Didicus caerulea*)
rhodanthe (*Helipterum manglesii*)
rose (*Rosa*)
safflower (*Carthamus tinctorius*)

sea holly *(Eryngium maritimum)*
sea lavender *(Statice latifolia)*
South Australian daisy *(Ixodia achilleoides)*
statice *(Limonium)*, all varieties
strawflowers *(Helichrysum)*
tansy *(Chrysanthemum vulgare)*
ti-tree *(Leptospermum)*
xeranthemum *(X. annum)*
yarrow *(Achillea)*

METHOD

Pick the flowers and foliage on a sunny day when they are in peak condition and not wet with dew. Select material that is free from pests and disease.

The air drying method can be done either by hanging or standing. For hanging, remove most of the foliage from the stems to ensure the drying process is quick. Group the stems into small bunches, then secure them to a coat-hanger with a rubber band, allowing the flower heads to hang freely.

The drying area must be airy, warm, dark and dry. It is an advantage to have an overhead rack for suspending the bunches from the hangers.

This is an effective method for a wide range of flowers, and many varieties of foliage are also dried successfully this way. Eucalyptus leaves from the *E. crenulata* and *E. cinerea* both dry to a lovely sage-blue colour. Bay leaves turn an attractive green, and many of the silver foliage plants, e.g., artemisia and lamb's tongue, retain their colour well.

The standing method of air drying involves standing the stems of the flowers or foliage in a container that has been weighted so that they remain upright during the drying process.

Flowers that can be dried in this position include baby's breath, hydrangeas, sea holly and many of the Australian natives, e.g., South Australian daisy, ti-tree, curry flower. Eucalyptus leaves and pussy willow in bud are just two of the types of foliage that can be dried using this method. The branches of foliage that are dried standing upright will change into interesting free-form shapes.

SILICA GEL DRYING

Silica gel is a chemical compound that has been used in industry for many years because of its ability to absorb moisture. It looks like fine blue sand when completely dry, but as it begins to absorb the moisture from the flowers, the colour changes to pink. You can use the gel again and again, but it must be dried in the oven or the microwave oven between each usage and stored in airtight containers when not needed.

Silica gel drying produces very clear, vivid colours, not always true to the original colour of the flower. Any shade of blue in a red or pink flower is likely to turn purple or mauve. Orange roses turn red and red roses turn almost black. Some white flowers retain their colour, others turn parchment. Greens stay green when first dried but lose colour rapidly when exposed to light.

Some leaves can be dried in silica gel successfully. The leaves retain their colour and form but become extremely brittle and must therefore be handled with care.

Those flowers and foliage that are well suited to silica gel drying include:

anemone (*Anemone* spp.)
carnation (*Dianthus*)
coneflower (*Rudbeckia*)
cornflower (*Centaurea cyanus*)
daffodil (*Narcissus*)
dahlia (*D. cultorum*)
delphinium (*D. hybridum*)
freesia (*F.* x *hybrida*)
gerbera (*Multisia*)
hellebores (*Helleborus* spp.)
heliopsis (*H. scabra*)
hollyhock (*Althaea rosea*)
jonquil (*Narcissus jonquilla*)
lemon leaves (*Citrus* spp.)
marigold (*Tagetes*)
nigella (*N. damascena*)
pansy (*Viola* x *wittrockiana* hybrids)
peony (*Paeonia*)
ranunculus (*Ranunculus* spp.)
rose (*Rosa*) and rose leaves
shasta daisy (*Chrysanthemum maximum*)

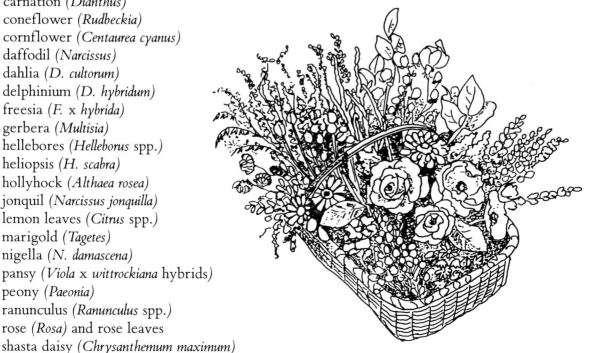

snapdragon *(Antirrhinums)*
strawberry leaves *(Fragaria)*
sunflower *(Helianthus)*
tulip *(Tulipia)*
violet *(Viola)*
zinnia *(Z. elegans)*

Because silica gel is a powdery substance and creates a dust when poured, it is wise to wear a mask and gloves at all times when working with the gel.

METHOD

Have all the equipment ready for use before you begin picking the flowers and foliage. This includes a variety of plastic airtight boxes, kitchen trays for sitting the boxes on when pouring the silica gel, a large kitchen spoon or scoop, and at least two 3 kg (6 lb) containers of silica gel.

There are certain things to remember when picking flowers and foliage for silica gel drying. They should be in perfect condition, because any bruising or insect damage becomes exaggerated during the drying process. Pick the flowers after the dew has dried but before the sun reaches its peak. There should be no trace of moisture on the surface of the petals but the flowers should be crisp, displaying their best form.

You should choose flowers in all stages of development — buds, partially opened and fully opened flowers. Plunge their stems into a bucket of water as you pick them, and only pick as many as you have time to process.

Once you've picked enough flowers, you must decide how they will maintain their shape best during the drying process. Should they lie face up or face down in the silica gel? Round, multi-petalled or cup-shaped flowers should be placed face up, and flat flowers, face down. Tall, spiked flowers and foliage should lie horizontally.

If you are using multi-petalled flowers, e.g. roses, the process is as follows. Make a bed of silica gel about 2–5 cm (1–2 inches) deep in an airtight box. Cut the stalks off and place the flowers face up on the silica gel, making sure that they do not touch the sides of the box or each other.

Using a spoon or scoop, surround each flower with enough silica gel to support the outer petals (Fig. 1). Carefully pour the silica gel between each layer of petals, separating some petals in the tighter flowers with your fingertips to make sure the silica gel trickles down. Keep a steady stream of silica gel moving gently over and between the flowers so that the level builds up evenly and a constant pressure is maintained above and below each petal. Completely cover the flowers and seal the box.

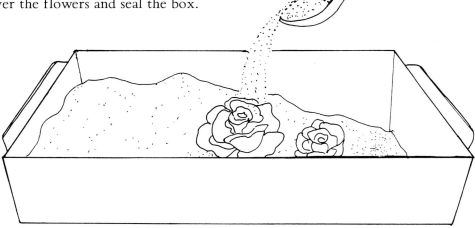

Figure 1

Flat-faced flowers, e.g. shasta daisies, should be dried face down over little mounds of silica gel placed in the airtight box (Fig. 2). In this way the flowers will maintain their natural shape, rather than being flattened under the pressure of the silica gel.

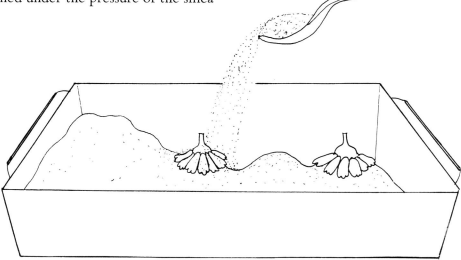

Figure 2

Spiky flowers, e.g. delphiniums, and foliage are laid out horizontally for drying. However, be careful not to lie them down against the base of the container, as this will flatten the underside of the flowers. To avoid this, build a series of supports from strips of cardboard notched at equal intervals and fit these tightly across the width of the box. Now rest the flowers on the supports, which are raised slightly above the bed of silica gel, and cover the entire flower with the silica.

Once you have covered the flowers and sealed the boxes, label each one, noting the type of flower and the date. The flowers must now be 'timed' and checked carefully to make sure that they do not become overly dry. If flowers are left in the silica gel for too long, they become very dehydrated and brittle. It is impossible to give an exact time for how long it takes each type of flower or foliage to dry, but most take between 3½ to 7 days. When the time comes to check their progress, gently pour off enough silica gel to expose the tips of a few flowers. If they feel crisp and dry, they are probably ready. If not, cover them again and let stand for a few more days.

If the flowers are ready, continue to gently pour off the silica gel into another container. You must be as careful during this process as you were when covering the flowers. Once the flowers are dry, they become brittle and will break easily. Avoid sudden movements during the pouring-off process and make sure that the silica gel doesn't fall back onto the freed petals, causing damage. Never try to pull the flowers straight out of the silica gel as you will lose petals.

Once the flowers have been removed, it is important to dust off any remaining silica gel using a soft artist's brush. Any small grains, because of their continuing absorbent qualities, will attract moisture from the atmosphere. This could result in a flower crumpling or collapsing in humid weather.

If the petals of some flowers are perfectly dry and papery but the stem and calyx remain moist, as often occurs with roses, remove them from the drying box. Then place them in another box in a bed of silica gel — push the stem and calyx deep into the silica while letting the petals remain uncovered. Seal the box and leave for several more days.

If you are not ready to arrange the flowers straight away, store them in an airtight box with a small amount of silica gel to keep the atmosphere dry. Flowers can be wired at this stage to make storing them easier (pages 23-4). When the glue you have used to attach the wire is completely dry, push the wired flowers into a thick layer of styrofoam or dry oasis at the bottom of the storage container, then add about half a cup of silica gel, making sure that the flowers are not touching.

Storing flowers that still retain some moisture will result in disaster — one damp flower will turn the entire box limp and discoloured.

This is the conventional method of using silica gel. However, there are two other methods — preheated silica gel drying and microwave oven or fast drying.

GLUING PRESERVED FLOWERS

Before you can use the silica-dried flowers, they must be glued. This gives stability to flowers — to roses in particular, as they are inclined to lose petals. Other flowers that may need to be glued are zinnias, shasta daisies, gerberas, carnations, marigolds, dahlias and hollyhocks, to name a few.

METHOD

Hold a single flower upside down and run a thin ribbon of transparent, fast-drying glue around the petals where they join the stem and centre of the flower (Fig. 3). Broken petals can also be glued on. For example, shasta daisies are inclined to lose petals and I often remake them almost entirely using this technique, with great success.

In some cases the petals can be glued to the calyx before the flower is dried. This is particularly effective with open roses if you run the glue deep into the flower. The gluing can also be done when the flowers are dry, but make sure that you use the glue sparingly so that it isn't too thick. In both

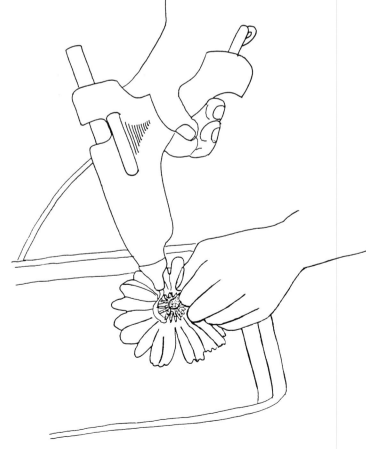

Figure 3

cases the glue must be completely dry before you either place the flowers in silica gel or store them.

WAXING PRESERVED FLOWERS

The most important part of preserving silica-dried flowers is the technique of waxing the flowers' backs. This results in them being totally supported, so that if they are exposed to humid conditions, they won't wilt. Most silica-dried flowers should be supported in this way, especially single-petalled varieties.

METHOD

Melt the wax to a point where it resembles clear water. I use white household candles melted in a tin, which sits inside a small saucepan of boiling water. Never melt wax without this water protection as it is flammable if overheated. Once it has melted, remove it from the heat and take it to your work area, which should be covered with newspaper.

Using a small paintbrush, carefully paint the backs of the flowers from the stem and calyx out to the tips of the petals (Fig. 4). Hold the flower upside down until dry. Repeat this process several times for each flower, always making sure that the wax doesn't drip onto the front of the flower.

ATTACHING FALSE STEMS

Because silica-dried flowers can rarely be dried with their natural stems, false stems must be added. These are made using either floral wire or a natural stem that has been dried separately.

METHOD

Wire stems should be constructed from lengths of either 0.7 mm (22 gauge) or 0.9 mm (20 gauge) wire. Using a hot glue gun, squeeze a small amount of glue into the hollow end of the flower's remaining stem, insert the wire and hold it in place

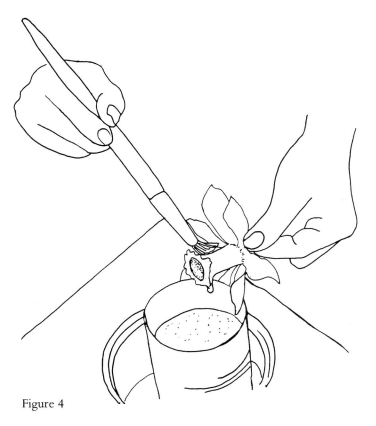

Figure 4

until dry. The area where the wire joins the stem should be covered with green parafilm (page 12).

Green parafilm can also be used to attach the wire without the need for glue. Hold the wire firmly next to the flower's remaining stem. Wrap the end of the green parafilm high up underneath the flower, covering both the wire and stem, and pull the tape firm (Fig. 5). Now turn the wire with the flower in one hand and wrap the parafilm around the wire in a downwards direction, stretching it slightly as you go (Fig. 6). If you wish to make the false stem longer, place a new length of wire beside the original wire, allowing a 2–5 cm (1–2 inch) overlap, and wrap the two together using the parafilm.

A dried, natural stem can be added to a flower that has had a wire stem glued into place. Make a clean cut at the top of the natural stem and insert the small wire stem into it. A small amount of clear, fast-drying glue will reinforce the join.

SEALING

Finally, before silica-dried flowers are ready to use, they should be sealed with a matt plastic spray. There are several on the market, e.g., 'Design Master's Super Surface Sealer', which are available from florist supply shops. These sprays protect the flowers from moisture and humidity and prevent wilting.

METHOD

Take the flowers outside on a windless, sunny day. Make sure that they are completely dry and free from silica gel crystals, and that your face is protected with a mask to avoid inhaling the fumes. Holding the can in an upright position about 12 cm (5 inches) from the flower's surface, spray with a smooth, side-to-side motion. This avoids spotting the flowers or causing them to sag with the weight of too much sealer. Two light coats are better than one heavy coat. Wait at least 30 minutes between applying coats.

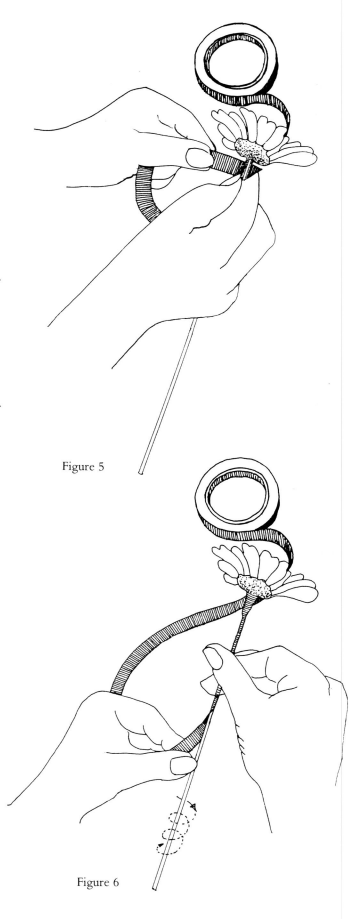

Figure 5

Figure 6

GLYCERINE PRESERVING

Glycerine is an excellent method for preserving many types of foliage. It has little in common with drying plant material, as instead of removing the moisture, the method involves replacing the moisture with glycerine. It is generally used for mature broad-leaved evergreens, but some varieties of flowers can be preserved successfully using this method.

Glycerine preserving involves a colour change which can range from gold to glossy green, brown to almost black. Foliage will last almost indefinitely and keep its three-dimensional form. If the leaves become dusty, they can be wiped with a damp cloth.

METHOD

The foliage to be used should be fully grown without blemishes and should be freshly picked. An ideal time for picking is at the end of summer to early autumn as most of the suitable foliage will be mature. If you would like to use autumn shades, pick just as the leaves begin to change colour. Remove any damaged leaves and wipe off debris with a damp cloth. Strip the leaves from the lower part of the stem so that they won't be under the glycerine and crush or split the woody stems, exposing the water-conducting tissue. This will make it easier for the stems to absorb the glycerine solution. Place prepared branches immediately into the warm solution, making sure that the stems are well covered.

To prepare the glycerine solution, combine two parts of warm water with one part glycerine and stir vigorously — glycerine is heavier than water, so a lot of effort is required to mix the two together. Pour the solution into a heavy upright container or a small bucket inside a larger bucket. Make sure that these containers are stable and won't fall over with the weight of the foliage.

Check the solution regularly to make sure the level is being maintained and add more when necessary. The time needed for this method varies from 4 days to 3 weeks. The leaves may at first look 'spotty', as though they have been splashed with oil. When the spots disappear and the leaf colouring is even, the leaves have reached saturation point. Their surface should feel oily, leathery and soft, but they should not exude droplets. If they do, it means that the foliage has been immersed for too long a period.

Foliage such as ivy and magnolia leaves should be completely immersed in a bath of the glycerine solution for 2–6 days. Once the leaves have changed colour, remove them from the solution, wash them in a mild detergent and lay flat on paper towelling to dry.

If you need to store the preserved foliage, it can either be hung in bunches from wire coat-hangers, or individual leaves can be packed flat in boxes.

The following are suitable for preserving using the glycerine method.

baby's breath *(Gypsophila paniculata)*
copper beech *(Fagus sylvatica 'cuprea')*
holly *(Aquifolium)*
honesty *(Lunaria rediulua)* — use glycerine when pods have formed
hydrangea *(Macrophylla)*
ivy *(Hedera)* — only in glycerine bath
magnolia *(Magnolia* spp.)
oak leaves *(Quercus)*
pin-oak leaves *(Quercus palastris)*
pittosporum *(Pittosporaceae)*
protea *(Proteaceae)*
Russian olive *(Eleaguus augustifolius)*
statice *(Limonium sinuatum)*
vibernum *(Carifoliaceae)*

PRESSING

This method is used solely for preserving foliage. The types of foliage suitable for pressing are those that are fairly flat when in their natural state, e.g. ferns and nandina. Material dried in this way often looks stiff and flat, so it is wise to mix it cleverly with other foliage in an arrangement. Try to collect a variety of shapes and colours. Grey-tinted leaves, e.g. cineraria, grey-leaved poplars and the grey herb wormwood look effective and don't change colour when pressed. Autumn foliage can also be successfully pressed, e.g. ornamental grape leaves. Cut them just as they turn yellow, orange, red and russet and they will retain their natural colours. Green foliage usually remains green, however the chlorophyll which gives the green colour disintegrates rapidly when exposed to either natural or artificial light. This foliage can be sprayed lightly with a natural green dye, e.g. 'Design Master' moss green, available from florist shops or florist supply companies.

METHOD

Pick the foliage when it is fresh and free from moisture and insect damage, and press straight away. Pressing should be done in a warm, dry room. It is unnecessary to press the foliage under a great weight. Simply spread several layers of newspaper and foliage.

The newspaper will absorb the moisture, and the loose arrangement of the pile will allow air to circulate, thus avoiding mildew. The leaves will be dry within 1–2 weeks, depending on their thickness. Check occasionally, lifting the leaves to make sure that they don't stick to the surface of the newspaper.

The following are suitable for pressing.
acanthus (*Acanthaceae*)
cineraria (*Senecio*)
columbine (*Aquelegia vulgaris*)
gradiolus leaves (*G. primulinus*)
grey-leaved poplars (*Solicaceae*)
iris leaves (*Germanica*)
lady's mantle (*Alchemilla mollis*)
maidenhair fern (*Adiantum*)
nandina (*N. domestica nandinaceae*)
ornamental grape (*Vitis*)
strawberry leaves (*Fragania*)
wormwood (*Artemisia absinthium*)

WIRING BUNCHES OF FLOWERS

Flowers, especially small flowers, can often look more effective in an arrangement when they are wired into bunches. They are also easier to handle this way.

METHOD

For this type of wiring, use a 0.55 mm (24 gauge) wire. Hold the flowers in one hand and place the wire vertically at the back of the stems. Bend both ends of the wire down to form a hairpin shape (Fig. 7). Then, holding the hairpin and stems firmly between your thumb and forefinger, wind the longer end of the wire around the shorter end and the stems two or three times. The long end, once straightened, now acts as the stem for the bunch (Fig. 8).

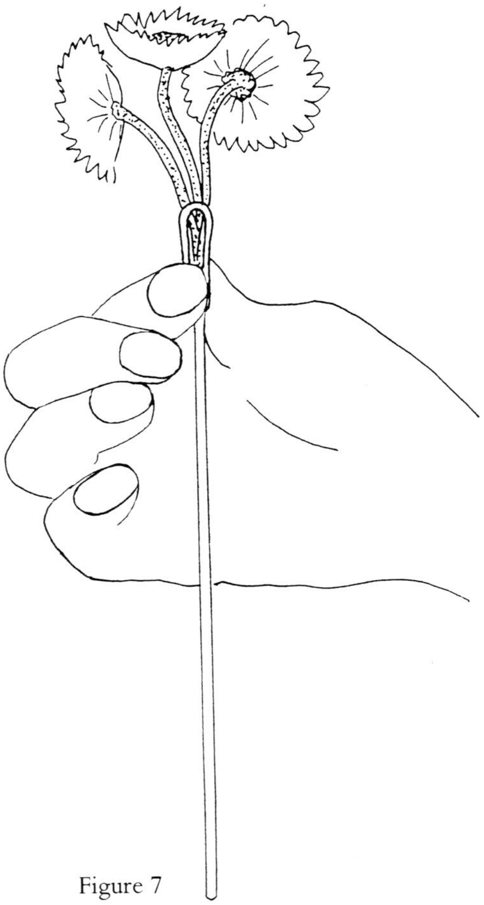

Figure 7

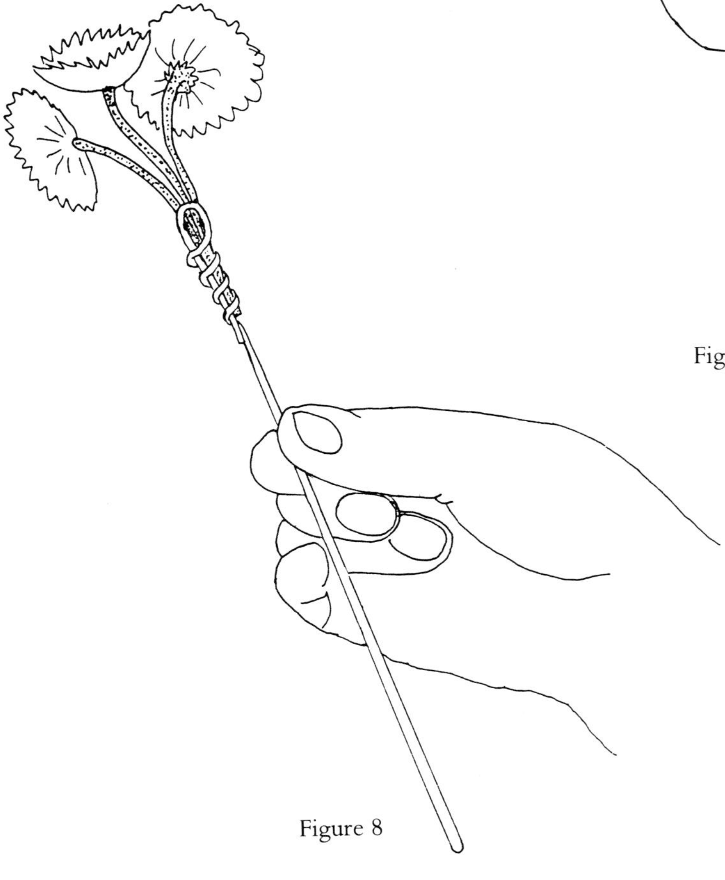

Figure 8

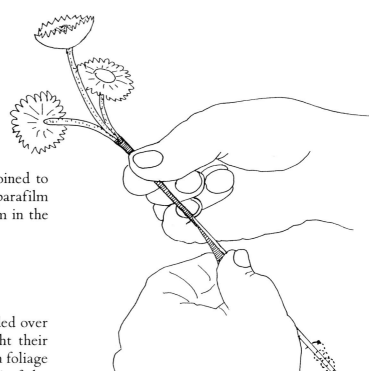

The area where the stems have been joined to the wire can be covered using some green parafilm (page 12). You can also cover the wire stem in the same way (Fig. 9).

ARTIFICIAL COLOURING

Because preserved flowers can become faded over time, it is sometimes necessary to highlight their colours, either by dyeing or spraying. Green foliage in particular benefits from spraying, as it fades quickly, eventually becoming beige or brown. Roses are also known to lose their vibrancy quite quickly, and so benefit from being treated occasionally.

In addition, by enhancing some of your filler materials with natural-looking colours, you can add greater vitality to your arrangements.

Figure 9

METHOD

'Design Master' is an excellent spray dye available in a can. There is an extensive colour range available, but when choosing be careful to select the more natural colours, as over-dyed and unnaturally coloured flowers look awful. Some colours that are suitable are: Moss Green, Celedon, Dusty Rose, Perfect Pink, Sonia, Yellowtint and Mauvetint. Make sure the flowers are clean and dry. When spraying, use even strokes, keeping the can about 60 cm (24 inches) from the flowers or foliage. Spray lightly, moving the can from side to side in a steady, continuous motion. 'Design Master' sprays are available from florist shops or florist supply companies.

Spray colouring can be effective but you must be careful not to overdo it. One light spray is enough — keep the can moving steadily from side to side all the time.

GROWING FLOWERS AND FOLIAGE FOR DRYING

There is something very satisfying about picking, drying and arranging flowers and foliage that you have grown yourself.

Over the past twenty years I have experimented with growing both traditional and native flowers in four different gardens with great success. The range of plants that can be used for drying is almost limitless. The choice you make about which plants to grow and use will depend on the conditions in your garden, e.g., the soil and the climate, and on the season.

It is quite easy to grow enough flowers to be able to harvest the quantity you need for drying without affecting the overall look of your garden. This can be achieved by mixing things up, by growing the plants you intend to use for drying in amongst plants that won't be used for this purpose. For example, put plants traditionally used for drying alongside other perennials and annuals in a mixed border; mix herbaceous plants with decorative shrubs and roses. This will help create a wonderful, year-round display.

However, if your enthusiasm for drying and arranging flowers increases and you need large quantities of flowers, it may be a good idea to have a separate garden, specially designed for that purpose, in an inconspicuous area. Gardens that are harvested heavily and continually don't look attractive.

Many of the flowers you will need can be grown in the spring by seeding directly into the ground once the fear of frosts has passed. Of course, there are some plants, such as larkspur (*Delphinium ujacis*) and sea holly (*Eryngium maritimum*), that need frosts and cold conditions for germination.

Below I have listed just a few of the flowers and foliage that I have grown and dried successfully for my flower arrangements. This is not meant to be an exhaustive list, but it will give you some ideas about which flowers you can grow that are suitable for drying, when and how to harvest them, and which method you should use to preserve them.

ACROCLINIUM (*Helipterum roseum*)

Acroclinium is an everlasting daisy in shades of pink and white with a yellow centre. Pick it when the flowers are in bud or just open and hang upside down in bunches to dry. It can be wired before drying by pushing a wire into the calyx of the flower. When the flower dries and shrinks, the flower will be held firmly in place.

AMMOBIUM DAISY (*A. alatum*)

This daisy is an Australian native which grows well in cold regions. It is easy to germinate from seed and although said to be an annual, it will survive for a couple of seasons. Pick the branches of daisies when the flowers are fully open and hang in bunches to dry.

BABY'S BREATH
(*Gypsophila paniculata*)

The double-flowering perennial varieties are the best. Pick when the flowers are at their peak and hang in bunches to dry. They can also be dried upright in a container and preserved in glycerine.

CHINESE LANTERN (*Physalis franchetii*)

This perennial is grown for its bright orange calyx. The calyces should be picked before being spoilt by autumn weather and hung in bunches to dry.

Grow this plant in a separate area of the garden as it can become invasive in a flower border.

DELPHINIUM (*D. hybridum*)

These flowers grow easily in good, rich soil. I usually germinate them in autumn, and by the following summer I have plants that are large enough to produce their first flowers. Pick when the flowers are nearly all open and hang in bunches to dry. They can also be dried successfully in silica gel.

GLOBE AMARANTH (*Gomphrena globosa*)

These clover-like flowers are relatively hardy annuals. They come in quite a variety of colours. They can be picked from midsummer onwards, the timing not being very important as their shape and colour change very little. Pick in bunches and hang to dry.

LONAS (*L. inodora*)

Lonas have clusters of yellow, ball-shaped flowers. Pick them when the flowers are mature and hang in bunches to dry.

LOVE-IN-A-MIST (*Nigella damascena*)

This is almost a weed in my garden, as it will seed itself everywhere once a couple of plants have been established. The lovely blue flower should be picked when fully open and dried in silica gel. The seed capsules can also be picked, when formed and still green, and hung to dry in bunches for use in arrangements.

RODANTHE *(Helipterum manglesii)*

This is a pink and white, soft everlasting daisy. They are difficult to grow in a cool temperate climate, the type of climate that I live in. I have also had mixed success in germinating them, so in recent times I have bought them fresh from flower markets. They should be picked when the flowers are open and hung in bunches to dry.

SEA HOLLY *(Eryngium* spp.*)*

I have grown at least three varieties of this perennial, *E. caeruleum, E. giganteum, E. yuccaefolium,* all of which can be dried successfully. Pick when the flowers are open and mature. You can hang them in bunches to dry or stand them upright in a container.

STATICE *(Limonium)*

There are many varieties, although I mainly grow the perennials, which have very delicate flowers. These include fairy statice sierra *(Limonium sinense)*, German statice *(L. dumosum)*, blue smoke statice *(S. penezii)*, white smoke statice *(S. tartarica),* sea lavender *(S. latifolia).* The flowers of the annual varieties are more tightly clustered. These include pink pokers *(S. suworowi)* and statice fortress *(S. sinuata)* and have a wonderful colour range — apricot, heavenly blue, dark blue, purple, rose, white and yellow. Both are easy to grow, and you can buy them in punnets from a nursery if you don't want large numbers. Pick when the flowers are fully open and hang in bunches for air drying.

It is also possible to preserve them using glycerine. This will stop the flowers from becoming brittle and falling, but the colour of the stem will change to brown.

STRAWFLOWER *(Helichrysum)*

These are available in a large range of shapes and colours, from the so-called 'Bikini' to the extra-large, mixed or single colour varieties. The flower buds should be picked just as they open but before the centre of the flower is showing.

The flowers can be dried on their natural stems by hanging them upside down in bunches. However, they tend to become very brittle and often fall off the stems. This can be avoided by wiring the flowers before drying, and as they dry, the flowers will shrink and tighten around the wire.

XERANTHEMUM *(X. annum)*

This is a pretty mauve, pink and cream daisy which thrives in poor, dry soil. Pick when the flowers are fully open and hang in bunches upside down to dry.

YARROW *(Achillea)*

The perennial varieties — 'Golden Plate', 'Coronation Gold' and *Achillea ptarmica* — all dry well when picked at their peak and hung upside down to dry. A recently released pink variety doesn't air-dry well, but it can be dried successfully using silica gel.

During spring I also plant many different flowers to be used for silica gel drying. These include:

CONEFLOWER *(Rudbeckia compositae)*

The many-petalled varieties, e.g. 'Goldilocks' and 'Double Gold' dry successfully in silica. Grow in late spring. Seedlings can be bought from most well stocked nurseries. Pick the flowers when dry and fully open, and place face-down over small mounds of silica and cover. Seal the box and dry — about seven days. When ready to use, glue and wax the backs of the petals for support.

DAFFODIL *(Narcissus)*

All daffodils are easy to grow but they prefer a climate that has cold winters. The single varieties are the most successful to dry, but you can dry them all. Bulbs can be bought from nurseries and planted in an open sunny position in March. Most bulbs are planted about three times their actual depth into average garden soil. Pick them when dry and in various stages — when buds, half open and fully open. Place them in a bed of silica and carefully cover them. Seal the container and leave to dry for approximately five days. When ready to use, wax the back of the petals and trumpet area for support.

DAHLIA *(D. cultorum)*

Some varieties can be grown as annuals from seed, but most are produced from a fleshy tuber. They can be bought from nurseries and the small to medium varieties are the most successful to dry and offer a wide range of colour. Pick when the flowers are fully open, dry and free from insect damage. These flowers are many petalled so place upright in a bed of silica, cover completely and seal the container. Leave to dry for five to seven days. When ready to use, wax the backs of the petals.

DOUBLE MIXED HOLLYHOCKS *(Althaea rosea)*

The double varieties are the ones that dry most successfully in silica. Germinate seeds either in boxes or directly into the ground once fear from frosts has passed. You can also buy punnets of seedlings from your local nursery. Pick the flowers when dry and fully open, and place in an upright position in a bed of silica. Cover carefully with silica, seal the box and leave to dry — about seven days. When ready to use, paint the backs of the petals with wax.

LEMON AND ORANGE MARIGOLDS (*Tagetes patula*)

The large African marigold which has big bold double flowers in orange, gold and lemon is one of the most successful for silica drying. You can germinate them directly into the ground in spring when the fear from frosts has passed, or buy seedlings in punnets from your local nursery. A few plants will provide you with many flowers. Pick the flowers mid-morning when they are free from moisture and place upright in a bed of silica gel. Completely cover with the silica, seal the box and leave until dry — about eight days. When ready to use, paint the backs of the petals with hot wax.

PANSY (*Viola* x *wittrockiana* hybrids)

They can be germinated from seeds in boxes during autumn and winter or bought as seedlings from your local nursery. A couple of punnets of seedlings will give you plenty of flowers to dry. Pick them when dry and fully open, and place them face down or up in silica — it doesn't seem to matter which way they dry, as they are flat-faced flowers. Cover them completely, seal the container and dry for approximately two to three days. When ready to use, wax the back of the petals.

RANUNCULUS (*Ranunculus* spp.) *and* ANENOME (*Anenome* spp.)

In a sunny position, plant the claws or pointed corms, which you can buy from your local nursery during February-April, with the 'points' down, 50 mm (about 2″) deep and 15 cm (6″) apart. Pick the flowers when open and dry. The single anemone will be dried face down over a small mound of silica, but the ranunculus is many petalled and will sit upright in a bed of silica. Cover completely, seal the container and dry for approximately seven to eight days.

ROSE *(Rosa)*

Roses are easy to grow and a few bushes will give you plenty of flowers for drying. Plant during the winter in an open sunny position and keep well watered. Most nurseries have a wide range of roses available from May onwards. Pick the roses when dry, at different stages — buds, half open and fully open. Leaves can also be picked when mature and not damaged by wind or insects. Place the roses upright in a bed of silica and cover completely. Seal boxes and leave to dry for approximately eight to ten days. Leaves will take less time. When ready to use, glue and wax the backs of the petals. The backs of the leaves can be waxed, but they are successful without wax.

SHASTA DAISY
(Chrysanthemum maximum)

This is a hardy perennial ranging from single flat-petalled and single frilled petals to double varieties. It will grow in most soils and in semi-shade as well as full sun. You can buy the plants from most well stocked nurseries or ask your friends for a couple of pieces with roots and plant during the winter in an area where there is room to spread. Pick the flowers at different stages — buds, half open to fully open — but don't pick old flowers as the yellow centres become dull. Pick when completely dry and before the hot sun has made the petals wilt. Dry in silica straight away by placing each flower over a small mound of silica at the bottom of the container and cover completely. I mostly dry the single flat-petalled varieties and these flowers dry a more natural shape when facing downwards. Seal the container and dry for about seven days. When ready to use the daisies, glue the petals and wax the back of each flower.

SUNFLOWER *(Helianthus)*

These are easy to grow from seeds in spring. They can be germinated directly into the ground in average garden soil in a sunny open position. The smaller varieties are the most successful for silica drying. Pick the flowers when dry and fully open, and place face down over a mound of silica. Cover completely, seal the container and leave to dry for about seven to ten days. When ready to use, glue and wax the backs of the petals.

TULIP *(Tulipia)*

Tulips can be planted from April to May. They are easy to grow in average garden soil in an open sunny position or can be successfully grown in pots. Buy the bulbs from your local nursery and plant about twice the depth of the bulb. The smaller varieties, single and double, are the most successful to dry in silica. Pick in spring when the flowers are open but not fully blown and are completely dry. Place carefully in a bed of silica and pour more silica inside the flower first and then around the outside, making sure that the flower petals don't flop before becoming completely covered. Seal the container and dry for approximately seven days. When ready to use, the flowers will need to be waxed on the outside of the petals.

ZINNIAS *(Z. elegans)*

The medium to small flat-petalled varieties are the ones that are most successfully dried in silica. You can germinate seed directly into the ground in spring once fear from frosts has passed, or buy seedlings in punnets from your local nursery. The flowers should be picked when dry and at different stages of development — when buds are half open and when fully open — but before the centres have begun to produce pollen. Place in an upright position in a bed of silica gel and cover completely. Seal the box and leave until dry — about seven days. When ready to use, glue and wax the backs of the petals for support

FOLIAGE

The following plants can be grown to provide greenery (filler) and seed heads:

acanthus *(Hungaricus)*

artemisia *(Artemisia albula)*

bells of Ireland *(Mollucella laevis)*

celosia *(Amaranthaceae)*

eucalyptus *(E. cinerea* and *E. crenulata)*

golden rod *(Solidago)*

green amaranth *(Amaranthus hypochondriacus)*

honesty *(Lunaria)*

lamb's tongue *(Stachys lanata)*

lavender *(Lavandula)*

leek heads *(Allium ampeloprasum* var. *porrum)*

lemon tree *(Citrus limon)*

oregano *(O. vulgare; labiata)*

pepper berries *(Schinus molle)*

pussy willow *(Salix caprea)*

rosemary *(Rosmarinus)*

scabiosa *(S. stellata)*

wild grasses: hare's tail *(Lagurus ovatus)*, and quaking grass *(Briza maxima)*

AUSTRALIAN NATIVES

If you don't have your own garden, its possible to buy supplies from the many florists, flower stalls and flower markets, which have an enormous range of flowers and foliage available these days. And even if you do have a garden, you'll possibly want to supplement the range that you grow by purchasing additional varieties.

Native flowers and foliage, which can be difficult or slow to grow, are now readily available in both fresh and dried form. Some of the natives that can be used to great effect in an arrangement include:

banksia *(B. baxterii, B. coccinea, B. hookerana and B. speciosa)*

billy buttons *(Craspedia globosa)*

cauliflower morrison *(Verticordia browneii)*

curry flower *(Lysinema ciliatum)*

feather flower *(Verticordia)*

golden cluster everlastings *(Sanfordia)*

sago bush *(Ozothamnus diosmisolia)*

silver hair *(Aotus carinata)*
soft white paper daisy *(Leucochrysum albicans)*
South Australian daisy *(Ixodia achilleoides)*
ti-tree *(Leptospermum)*
woolly bush *(Adenanthos cygnorum)*
yellow helichrysum *(Bracteantha viscosa)*

i.   Arranging daffodils in silica gel for drying
ii. Pouring silica gel over and between the flowers
iii. Dried daffodils; note that the silica gel has now turned pink
iv. Equipment used for waxing and wiring

i

ii

iii

iv

Facing Arrangement in Mauve and Pink of delphiniums, larkspur, snapdragons, lily buds, statice, daisies, roses, tulips

Daffodils, tulips, gerberas, marigolds, shasta daisies and dahlias feature in this Large Mixed Table Arrangement with delphiniums, larkspur, s ice, daisies, Billy buttons and globe amaranths

Shasta daisies, tulips, gerberas and marigolds are the focal points of this Table Centre Arrangement, which also include strawflowers, pepper berries, Billy buttons, larkspur, delphiniums, lavender and statice

Autumnal Arrangement of Zinnias in red and yellow

Rose Arrangement in Antique Vase features both old-fashioned and hybrid roses

Shasta daisies and wild grasses are used to create a rustic effect in this Basket Arrangement

Wall Hanging of rosebuds and peonies, strawflowers, larkspur, ti-tree, pepper berries and statice

Detail of Wall Hanging

Detail of Loose Posy

Harkening from the Elizabethan and Victorian eras, this Tussie Mussie is a nosegay of roses, strawflowers, pepper berries, larkspur, lavender, rosemary, hydrangea, lamb's tongue, tarragon, oregano and sage

Decorated hat featuring a garland of roses, daisies, maidenhair fern, baby's breath, lavender, strawflowers, delphiniums, statice, larkspur, ti-tree and pepper berries

Eucalyptus leaves form the base of this Wreath of roses, daisies, larkspur, strawflowers and statice

This pretty Loose Posy is a colourful array of roses, tulips, lavender, larkspur, delphiniums, statice, daisies, hydrangea, strawflowers and baby's breath

Arranging Dried Flowers

It is important not to feel too restricted by rules when arranging dried flowers. There are just a few general guidelines which you may find helpful to keep in mind.

Before you begin, it is important that you try to visualise how you want the arrangement to look. This will allow you to work to a plan. Much will depend on the flowers and foliage that you are intending to use and where the arrangement is to be situated in the room.

Make sure that the height and the width of your arrangement is in proportion to the vase — approximately one and a half to two times the height of the vase for both the height and the width.

It is always more pleasing to the eye to see uneven numbers. This relates particularly to Focal Point Flowers, the most important flowers in an arrangement. For these, you should use three or five of the same type of flower.

Group your colours, bringing them up through the arrangement in flowing and gradual lines. This looks more effective than spotting different colours randomly throughout the arrangement. Also, keep the open, heavier looking flowers towards the centre, on short stems.

There are a number of things you can do to enhance the sense of the naturalness of your arrangement. Keep the outline free-flowing and avoid stiff triangular shapes. Remember to use a mixture of buds, half-opened flowers and open flowers, and include plenty of greenery with your flowers to generate a feeling of freshness.

Another way to create a natural look is to use flowers of different stem lengths next to each other, so that the light can penetrate to different depths.

The stems should appear to radiate from the centre, in a way that is reminiscent of most growing plants. Never cross the stems.

When you have finished, always stand back and examine the arrangement carefully from all sides. Check that the flowers have been distributed evenly and that there are no gaping holes.

LINE ESTABLISHING FLOWERS

These are flowers that generally have a spike-form or an elongated spray form, e.g. lavender, salvia, delphinium, larkspur, snapdragon, curry flower, fine ti-tree, golden rod, some forms of perennial statice and achillea, just to name a few.

They are used to strengthen the outline of the arrangement, which has previously been formed using the foliage, grasses and sometimes seed pods, and to create a pleasing overall shape. You will also be establishing the height and width of the arrangement with these flowers.

FILLER FLOWERS

These are the flowers that give body to the arrangement. They create the depth and contrast and also add to the shape; examples include annual statice, ixodia, hydrangea, strawflowers, sago bush, cauliflower morrison, coarse ti-tree and pepper berries, just to name a few. Small filler flowers, e.g. soft white paper daisies, rhodanthe and xeranthemum, can add vitality to the arrangement with their different and interesting shapes.

FOCAL POINT FLOWERS

These are the centre-of-interest flowers, many being round in form, and they are the largest flowers in the arrangement, e.g. roses, dahlia, zinnia, peony, shasta daisy, gerbera, protea, banksia and sunflowers.

These flowers are used to attract and hold attention. It is particularly pleasing to the eye to

see a few special flowers placed centrally and quite close together, preferably in uneven numbers. Often they are the most fragile flowers and should be added to the arrangement right at the end when the main working of the arrangement is completed.

CARING FOR YOUR ARRANGEMENTS

Because dried flowers are delicate and brittle, they require special conditions if you hope to keep your arrangements looking bright and attractive. Here are some suggestions to help prolong their life.

- Never expose your arrangements to bright sunlight, heat or fluorescent lighting. This will result in brittleness and loss of colour very quickly.

- Keep your arrangements away from humidity and draughts. For example, bathrooms and kitchens aren't the ideal places. The flowers will take up moisture and become limp, shapeless and sometimes mouldy.

- Spray your arrangements regularly, preferably outdoors on a windless, sunny day, with a clear matt sealer. This will form a barrier on the surface of the petals and leaves and prevent moisture from penetrating. It will also help to make the whole arrangement look fresher. Remember not to spray too closely or too thickly as this can give the flowers a glossy and plastic appearance.

- It is possible to dust arrangements with a soft watercolour paintbrush. With patience, you can remove most of the dust and loose petals by gently shaking and blowing the arrangement. It is advisable to do this outdoors. Never use a vacuum cleaner — you may lose the whole arrangement.

- Watch out for insect damage, indicated by petals dropping and the centres of flowers disintegrating. Roses and some of the soft varieties of everlasting daisies are susceptible to moth infestations. As a precaution, place dried flowers that you are about to use in the freezer for 24 hours — below zero temperatures will kill any infestation.

■ Dried flowers do not last forever. Remember to remove your arrangements before they become brown and dusty. An arrangement that uses silica-dried flowers will keep its colour and fresh appearance for at least 6 months. After that, there will be a slow loss of colour, usually beginning with the foliage. The more fragile the flower, the quicker it will deteriorate.

Mauve and Pink Facing Arrangement

REQUIREMENTS
Blue-grey glazed ceramic bowl
Dry oasis
Dry sand or stones
Hot glue gun and glue sticks
0.7 mm (22 gauge) green floral wire
Green parafilm and green florist's tape
Wire-cutters
Secateurs

Foliage:
Myrtle *(Myrtus)*, air-dried (1)
Ivy *(Adiantum)*, glycerined (2)
Nandina *(Nancinaceae)*, glycerined or pressed (3)
Silver hair foliage *(Aotus carinata)*, air-dried (4)

Line Establishing Flowers:
Pale blue delphiniums *(D. hybridum)*, air-dried (5)
Cream and pink larkspur *(Delphinium ujacis)*, air-dried (6)
Cream and pink snapdragons *(Antirrhinum)*, silica-dried (7)

Filler Flowers:
Mauve-pink lily buds *(Lilium)*, silica-dried (8)
Dusty pink statice *(Limonium)*, air-dried (9)
Purple and mauve larkspur *(D. ujacis)*, air-dried (10)
Pink rhodanthe daisies *(Helipterum manglesii)*, air-dried (11)

Focal Point Flowers:
Pink roses *(Rosa)*, silica-dried (12)
Pale pink double tulips *(Tulipia)*, silica-dried (13)
Mauve-pink single tulips *(Tulipia)*, silica-dried (14)
Deep pink gerberas *(Multisia)*, silica-dried (15)
Cream gerberas *(Multisia)*, silica-dried (16)

PREPARATION

Ensure that all the flowers and foliage have been dried by the appropriate method, and that their stems are firmly attached. Also, any gluing, waxing and sealing should have been completed for those flowers that require such treatment.

METHOD

- Fill the bottom of the vase with dry sand or stones so that the arrangement won't be top-heavy when completed. Cut a piece of dry oasis to fit the vase. It needs to rise 2.5 cm (1″) above the rim. Cut the pointy corners, making it a rounded shape.

- Cover the oasis with greenery, e.g. hydrangeas, by pinning it on with short pieces of 0.7 mm (22 gauge) green wire bent into a hairpin shape.

- Create an outline for the arrangement using the foliage, starting three-quarters of the way back in the vase, so that the foliage is leaning slightly backwards. The height and width of the arrangement should be in proportion to the vase — roughly one and a half to two times the height of the vase. However, don't feel too constricted by rules. In time you will develop an eye for what looks right. Try to make your background shape an easy flowing line, with no suggestion of stiffness.

  Choose two interestingly curved pieces of foliage for the sides and three smaller pieces to hang down over the front of the vase. Add a few large leaves to the centre for depth.

Almost all stems should be inserted at an angle
so that the overall effect is of flowers and
foliage radiating from the centre. They must
not cross.

The height and width of the arrangement should be in
proportion to the vase

Creating an outline using foliage

Line Establishing Flowers

■ Begin placing the Line Establishing Flowers in the arrangement. Choose a tall flower for the centre and two similar flowers, both a little shorter, and place them in front of the foliage so that they are leaning slightly backwards at an angle. Continue to place the pale blue delphiniums and pink and cream larkspurs at intervals around the outline and throughout the arrangement. Choose soft, flowing pieces for the sides and front, making sure that they come well over the rim of the vase.

■ Now the Filler Flowers can be added. Place them throughout the arrangement, working the shorter stemmed flowers down through the middle and towards the front to fill the vase and provide a contrast in shape and texture. Have flowers of different lengths next to each other to create a more natural and three-dimensional effect.

■ The Focal Point Flowers should now be inserted. As it is more pleasing to the eye to use uneven numbers, begin with five pink roses, keeping them close to the centre of the arrangement. Continue adding the other Focal Point Flowers. Distribute the tulips gracefully through the arrangement, and lastly, insert the dark-centred cream and pink gerberas. These will give a striking effect when placed in the central area, particularly if the deep pink gerberas are pushed well into the arrangement to give added depth, and one is made to hang well down over the front of the vase.

■ To lighten the arrangement's overall outline, I add mauve-pink lily buds and pink helipterum daisies, wired in bunches.

LARGE ROUND ARRANGEMENT

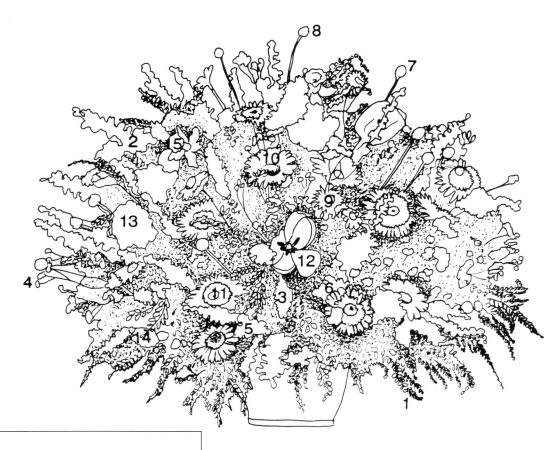

REQUIREMENTS

Green pottery vase
Dry oasis
Dry sand or stones
Hot glue gun and glue sticks
0.7 mm (22 gauge) green floral wire
Green parafilm and green florist's tape
Wire-cutters
Secateurs

Foliage:

Maidenhair fern (*Adiantum capillus-veneris*), pressed (1)

Line Establishing Flowers:
Blue delphiniums *(D. hybridum)*, air-dried (2)
Cream and pink larkspur *(Delphinium ujacis)*, air-dried (3)
White smoke statice *(Limonium tartarica)*, air-dried (4)

Filler Flowers:
Pink, purple and lemon statice *(Sinuata)*, air-dried (5)
Pink and white South Australian daisy *(Ixodia achilleoides)*, air-dried (6)
Yellow Billy buttons *(Craspedia globosa)*, air-dried (7)
Red and orange globe amaranth *(Gomphrena globosa)*, air-dried (8)
Acroclinium daisies *(Acroclinium roseum)*, air-dried (9)

Focal Point Flowers:
Shasta daisies *(Chrysanthemum maximum)*, silica-dried (10)
Yellow, pink, white and orange gerberas *(Multisia)*, silica-dried (11)
Yellow tulips *(Tulipia)*, silica-dried (12)
Marigolds *(Tagetes)*, silica-dried (13)
Lemon dahlias *(Dahlia cultorum)*, silica-dried (14)
Daffodils *(Narcissus)*, silica-dried (15)

PREPARATION

Dry the flowers and foliage and have them ready to use. The dahlias and shasta daisies in particular will need to be waxed, glued, sealed and wired.

METHOD

Fill the bottom of the vase with dry sand or stones. Cut a piece of dry oasis to fit the vase, making sure that the oasis extends 2.5 cm (1″) above its rim. With a knife, cut off the sharp corners and round the top and sides. Tape the top of the oasis to the sides of the vase, just below the outside rim.

- Cover the oasis with greenery, e.g., moss, hydrangeas or ferns, pinned on with pieces of 0.7 mm (22 gauge) wire bent into hairpin shapes.

- Make an outline using five to seven pieces of maidenhair fern, all of about the same length, arranged evenly around the edge of the vase. The width of the arrangement should be about the same as the height. Strengthen the outline by placing slightly shorter pieces of fern in between. Place a piece of fern in the centre that is approximately one and a half to two times the height of the vase. Work down from this point with more fern until you are satisfied with the overall shape.

- Add the Line Establishing Flowers. Start with about seven pieces placed around, and flowing over, the rim of the vase. Insert the lightest and most feathery pieces, e.g. white smoke statice, in the central top section. Continue adding the fern, working your way down from the top.

- The heavier Filler Flowers can now be added in between the Line Establishing Flowers to give the arrangement depth and contrast. Make sure that some of these flowers are placed deep in the centre of the arrangement. If you are using any of the everlasting daisies, such as the acroclinium daisies, they can be added at this stage. Keep the smaller flowers in the central top area, while mixing the medium to large flowers down through the arrangement. Place some around the edge of the vase so that they extend over the rim in an irregular line. Smaller daisies can be wired in bunches.

- Add the Focal Point Flowers. The round flowers, e.g., the dahlias and shasta daisies, are usually the dominant flowers in this arrangement. These blooms are quite fragile, and are the last to be added so that there is less chance of them being damaged. Use uneven numbers.

- Group the colours, bringing them up through the arrangement in flowing lines. This looks more effective than spotting colour all over the place. Also, the darker colours look better placed deep in the arrangement.

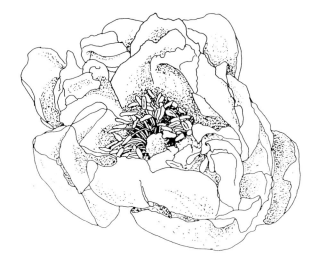

TABLE CENTRE ARRANGEMENT

If this arrangement is to be used for a dining table, it's important that it is the correct height, so that the flowers won't interfere with the guests' vision. The centre flowers should be no more than approximately 25 cm (10″) in height.

REQUIREMENTS
Low, round, dark green pottery vase
Dry oasis
Oasis prong and oasis fix
Hot glue gun and glue sticks
0.7 mm (22 gauge) green floral wire
Green parafilm and green florist's tape
Wire-cutters
Secateurs

Foliage:
Maidenhair fern (*Adiantum capillus-veneris*), pressed (1)

Line Establishing Flowers:
Deep blue and pink larkspur (*Delphinium ujacis*), air-dried (2)
Deep blue delphiniums (*D. hybridum*), air-dried (3)
Deep blue lavender (*Nana atropurpurea*), air-dried (4)
White smoke statice (*Limonium tartarica*), air-dried (5)

Filler Flowers:
White South Australian daisy (*Ixodia achilleoides*), air-dried (6)
Yellow, orange and pink strawflowers (*Helichrysum*), air-dried (7)
Pink pepper berries (*Schinus molle*), air-dried (8)
Small yellow Billy buttons (*Craspedia globosa*), air-dried (9)

Focal Point Flowers:
Shasta daisies (*Chrysanthemum maximum*), silica-dried (10)
Double yellow tulips (*Tulipia*), silica-dried (11)
Deep pink gerberas (*Multisia*), silica-dried (12)
Orange marigolds (*Tagetes*), silica-dried (13)

PREPARATION

Ensure that the flowers and foliage have been dried appropriately, and that all waxing, gluing, sealing and wiring has been completed.

METHOD

- Cut a piece of dry oasis to fit the vase. Attach an oasis prong, using oasis fix, to the bottom of the vase. Push the dry oasis firmly into position, so that it extends about 2.5 cm (1″) above the rim of the vase. With a knife, cut off the sharp corners and round the top and sides. At several points, tape the top of the oasis to the sides of the vase, below the outside rim.

■ Cover the oasis with greenery, pinned down with pieces of 0.7 mm (22 gauge) wire bent into small hairpin shapes.

■ Make an outline with the maidenhair fern similar to that used for the Large Round Arrangement (page 51). Use longer pieces at the sides to form a low oval shape, while the taller foliage should be no higher than 25 cm (10"). Fill in the outline with the fern, making a pleasing overall shape.

■ Add the Line Establishing Flowers, followed by the Filler Flowers, working in the same way as you did for the Large Round Arrangement, with the exception that the flowers must be kept much lower.

■ The Focal Point Flowers can now be added. The colour should be carried through from side to side, with any particularly special flowers, e.g., the yellow double tulips, facing outwards on all sides so that all the guests around the table have a pleasant view.

ROSE ARRANGEMENT IN ANTIQUE VASE

REQUIREMENTS

Antique glass vase — any lovely old vase can be used (roses look especially attractive in old silver vases)

Dry oasis

Oasis prong and oasis fix

Hot glue gun and glue sticks

Green parafilm and green florist's tape

0.7 mm (22 gauge) green floral wire

Wire-cutters

Secateurs

Matt spray sealer

Foliage:

Rose leaves, silica-dried

Flowers:

Old-fashioned and modern hybrid roses (*Rosa*), silica-dried — use as many varieties as you have available. I have used soft yellows through to peach pinks

PREPARATION

Over spring, summer and autumn, you will need to dry many different varieties of roses at different stages of development, which can then be stored until you are ready. If the arrangement is a round one, I use over six dozen roses.

All the roses need to be glued, waxed, wired and sealed before they can be used. It is important to follow the procedures carefully if you want your rose arrangement to last for any length of time.

METHOD

- Attach an oasis prong to the bottom of the vase with oasis fix. Cut a piece of dry oasis to fit the vase and push it firmly into position.

- Cover the oasis with a layer of green hydrangea flower heads or other greenery pinned down with short pieces of 0.7 mm (22 gauge) wire bent into hairpin shapes. Push the hydrangea around the sides of the oasis, making sure that none of the oasis can be seen through the glass vase.

Outline for a round rose arrangement

- Arrange the wired rose leaves around the edge of the vase, with some of them spilling over the edge in a natural way. Place a few leaves in the centre to establish the height of the arrangement, and some deep down to give a fuller effect. Make a pleasing overall shape with the remaining leaves.

- Use some of the small roses and buds as outline flowers and a single bud along with several small roses as the centre flowers. Continue adding small roses and buds.

- Fill in the general shape you have created using the medium to large roses. Remember that no two roses, when placed side by side, should have stems of the same length. By having a variety of rose types, e.g., old-fashioned and modern hybrids, you will provide the arrangement with contrasts of shape and texture. At this stage it is important not to touch the roses too frequently, and each new rose inserted must be handled with care. They are extremely fragile and it is surprisingly easy to break off a leaf or a petal. If this does happen, glue them back into place with the hot glue gun.

ZINNIA ARRANGEMENT

REQUIREMENTS

Small, terracotta pink, urn-shaped vase
Dry oasis
Hot glue gun and glue sticks
0.7 mm (22 gauge) green floral wire
Green parafilm
Wire-cutters
Secateurs

Foliage:
Red nandina *(Nandinaceae)*, microwave-dried
or pressed

Flowers:
Zinnias *(Z. elegans)*, silica-dried

PREPARATION

The zinnias should be silica-dried, their petals glued
around the calyx area and their backs waxed. False
stems of green 0.7 mm (22 gauge) wire need to
be added.

The microwave drying method involves the red
nandina foliage being dried between sheets of paper
towelling for 1 minute in a microwave oven set
on high. Wire the foliage if longer stems are
needed. In some cases two or three pieces can be
wired together.

METHOD

■ Cut a piece of dry oasis to fit the vase firmly.

■ Cover the oasis with zinnia heads, pinned on with short pieces of wire bent into hairpin shapes. I use lower quality zinnia heads that have been silica-dried, so that they still retain their brightness and make a wonderful bed of colour under the arrangement.

■ Choose the smaller to medium-sized flowers to make an overall shape. Keep in mind the size of the vase when establishing the height and width of the arrangement. The foliage can also be added at this stage — attractive curved pieces can be placed out on the edges and in amongst the zinnias to soften the overall effect. Place the larger and the dark-coloured zinnias well down in the arrangement to give a feeling of depth.

BASKET ARRANGEMENT

REQUIREMENTS

Rustic brown, pussy willow basket
Dry oasis
Hot glue gun and glue sticks
0.7 mm (22 gauge) green floral wire
Wire-cutters
Secateurs

Foliage:
A collection of wild grasses

Flowers:
Shasta daisies (*Chrysanthemum maximum*), silica-dried

PREPARATION

When selecting the shasta daisies for drying, try to pick them at different stages of development — some only just open, some half open, and some fully open. The backs of the petals of the silica-dried daisies will need to be glued to the calyx, and once the glue has dried, the back of each flower must be waxed.

METHOD

- Cut the dry oasis to fit firmly inside the basket.
- Cover the oasis completely with a layer of maidenhair fern, hydrangea, moss or whatever you have available. Pin down with short pieces of wire bent into hairpin shapes, making sure that the oasis is completely covered.

- Arrange the wild grasses, e.g., wild oats (*Avena fatua*), quaking grass (*Briza maxima*), in the basket in such a way as to create a slightly wild and informal effect. I choose grasses in shades of pale green.

- Add the shasta daisies. Arrange them freely in the basket, making some of the smaller daisies stand the tallest in the arrangement, while some of the larger, well-opened daisies sit deep in the basket. Also place some well-opened flowers so that they protrude over the edge of the basket.

- Don't overfill the basket. Rather, try to keep it looking as natural as possible. This can be achieved by never placing two daisies of the same height side by side and never having all the daisies' faces looking in the one direction.

STICK WALL-HANGING

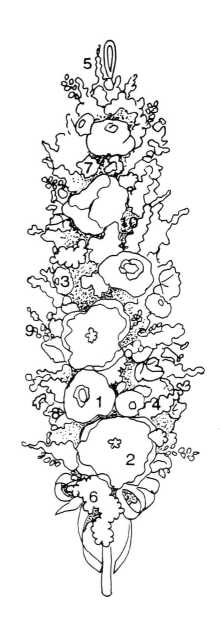

REQUIREMENTS

60 cm (24″) piece of thin bamboo
1.25 cm (½″) wide deep pink satin ribbon
Hot glue gun and glue sticks
0.24 mm (32 gauge) green floral wire
Wire-cutters
Secateurs

Focal Point Flowers:
Three pink rosebuds, varying sizes, silica-dried (1)
Three single peonies (*Paeonia lutea ludlowii*), silica-dried (2)

Filler Flowers:
Five pink strawflowers (*Helichrysum*), air-dried (3)
Deep pink larkspur (*Delphinium ujacis*), air-dried (4)
Pink ti-tree (*Leptospermum*), air-dried (5)
Pepper berries (*Schinus molle*), air-dried (6)
Pink and white statice (*Statice sinuata* and *Limonium sinense*), air-dried (7)

Foliage:
Ivy (*Hedera*), glycerined (8)
Myrtle (*Myrtus*), air-dried (9)
Hydrangeas (*Saxifragaceae*), air-dried (10)

PREPARATION

Ensure that the flowers and foliage have been dried appropriately, and that all waxing, gluing, sealing and wiring has been completed.

METHOD

- Attach the ribbon to the top of the bamboo stick using the hot glue gun. Make a 7 cm (3″) loop with the ribbon for hanging. Glue the back of the ribbon with the hot glue gun and twist it down the stick so that there is about a 1 cm (½″) space between each twist of ribbon. As you near the bottom of the stick, the spacing becomes narrower until the ribbon overlaps, covering the bamboo completely. To finish off, twist the ribbon evenly back up the bamboo stick for about 20 cm (8″), cut it and glue the end in place neatly. This forms the stalk of the hanging and will be seen when the hanging is complete.

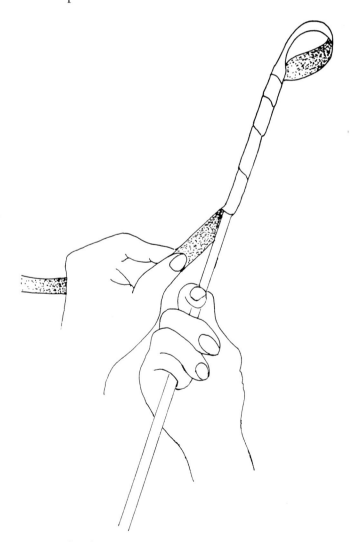

Covering bamboo stick with ribbon

- Using light pieces of foliage, sprigs of fine white statice, larkspur buds, sprigs of ti-tree and strawflower buds, make a small mixed bunch. Attach this about 5 cm (2″) from the top of the bamboo stick so that the top of the bunch doesn't reach very far above the bottom of the loop of ribbon. Bind firmly in place with the 0.24 mm (32 gauge) wire.

- Continue binding flowers and foliage onto the bamboo stick, making sure that you cover the sides but not the back of the stick, which should be flat so that it will hang correctly. As you continue down the stick, keep the light pieces of foliage and the flowers along the outside edges, choosing those pieces that curve interestingly to soften the outline. The hanging will look more effective if you leave at least 10 cm (4″) of the ribbon-covered stick showing at the base.

- The Focal Point Flowers are placed down the centre, starting with the smaller flowers and finishing with the largest, most beautiful peony.

- Arrange Filler Flowers such as the pink statice, pieces of larkspur, strawflowers, pepper berries and hydrangeas in and around the Focal Point Flowers, giving the arrangement depth so that it won't look flat

- Finish the wall-hanging by making a small bunch of pepper berries and ivy. Using the hot glue gun, glue a covering of flowers into place where the last few stems have been bound onto the stick. Finish off with a bow.

Small bunch of flowers attached to bamboo stick using binding wire

REATH

REQUIREMENTS

Vine wreath base — either buy or make this yourself

Hot glue gun and glue stick

Foliage:

Argyle apple eucalyptus *(E. crenulata)* or other variety, air-dried (1)

Focal Point Flowers:

Five peach-pink roses *(Rosa)*, silica-dried (2)

Five shasta daisies *(Chrysanthemum maximum)*, silica-dried (3)

Line Establishing Flowers:

Cream larkspur *(Delphinium ujacis)*, air-dried (4)

Filler Flowers:

Peach-pink strawflowers *(Helichrysum)*, air-dried (5)

Peach-pink South Australian daisies *(Ixodia achilleoides)*, air-dried (6)

Pale blue native statice *(Limonium)*, air-dried (7)

PREPARATION

Ensure that the flowers and foliage have been dried using the appropriate method and that they are ready to use. In particular, the shasta daisies will need to have been glued and waxed and sealed. The roses will also need to be sealed.

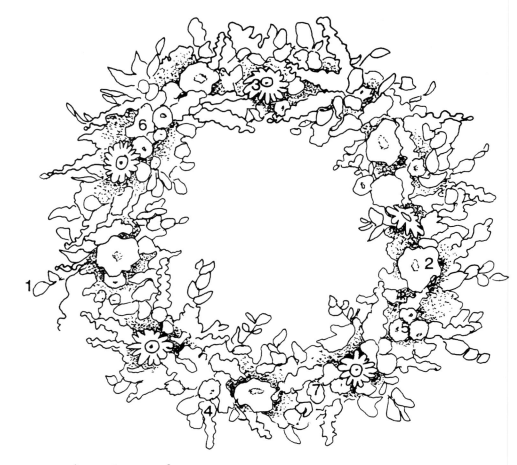

METHOD

- Using the hot glue gun, glue pieces of eucalyptus foliage over the vine wreath base.

- Now apply the hot glue to the base of each cream larkspur and gently press them into the eucalyptus foliage in groups of three. Place the larkspur in random directions and at slightly different depths. Lift the eucalyptus slightly as you go so that the larkspur almost appears to be growing out of the foliage naturally. The finished wreath looks more effective if they point in different directions.

- Add the Filler Flowers, gluing them throughout the foliage at even intervals to give a balanced effect. Use a variety of sizes and aim to create a sense of varying textures.

- Glue the Focal Point Flowers evenly along the mid-line of the wreath so that the overall effect is balanced. Make sure that some of these larger flowers are placed deep in amongst the eucalyptus foliage and not all of them are facing the same way.

DECORATED HAT

REQUIREMENTS

Plain straw or raffia hat
0.7 mm (22 gauge) green floral wire, 35 cm (14″) long
0.2 mm (36 gauge) green floral binding wire
Hot glue gun and glue sticks
Green parafilm and green florist's tape
Wire-cutter
Secateurs
95 cm (1 yard) of 1.25 cm (½″) wide deep pink satin ribbon

Flowers and Foliage:

Maidenhair fern (*Adiantum capillus-veneris*), microwave-dried or pressed (1)
Roses (*Rosa*), silica-dried (2)
Small acroclinium daisies, air-dried (*Acroclinium roseum*) (3)
Soft white paper daisies (*Leucochrysum albicans*), air-dried (4)
Baby's breath (*Gypsophila paniculata*), air-dried (5)
Lavender (*Lavandula*), air-dried (6)
Strawflowers (*Helichrysum*), air-dried (7)
Delphiniums (*D. hybridum*), air-dried (8)
South Australian daisies (*Ixodia achilleoides*), air-dried (9)
Statice (*Limonium sinuata*), air-dried
Rhodanthe daisies (*Helipterum sanfordii*), air-dried
Larkspur (*Delphinium ujacis*), air-dried
Ti-tree (*Leptospermum*), air-dried
Pepper berries (*Schinus molle*), air-dried

PREPARATION

Have all your flowers and foliage dried, wired, glued and sealed if necessary.

METHOD

■ Make a frame by joining two 0.7 mm (22 gauge) pieces of wire together which are both 35 cm (14″) long. Overlap them by 2-5 cm (1-2″) at the centre of the join. Bind them together with 0.2 mm (36 gauge) binding wire and cover the bound area with green parafilm. Put the wire frame on a round object so that it forms a circular shape. Fold back the ends of the wire to make two small hooks at either end of the frame. Check the size of the frame on the hat to make sure it will sit comfortably around the base of the crown. If it isn't large enough, simply add another piece of wire at one end.

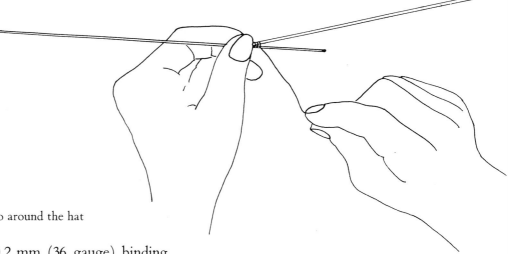

Making the wire frame to go around the hat

■ Attach a piece of 0.2 mm (36 gauge) binding wire to the left-hand hook and use this to bind a small bunch of foliage, baby's breath and a few small daisies together. Continue around the frame in this way, attaching each flower and small pieces of foliage securely. Because some of the daisies and most of the silica-dried flowers will have been wired already, you can let the false stems remain flat on the frame until a few have accumulated. Then cut the ends off to keep the garland neat and avoid bulkiness, and remove any sharp wires. The flowers should sit flat at the top and a little over the sides of the frame, and should be placed very close together so that they are all going in the same direction. Mix the different flowers with the baby's breath to keep the garland looking light and natural. Small flowers can be wired on in groups of three. Tiny bunches of wired pepper berries also look effective. The width of the garland is usually about two flowers across, but there are no set rules, and it's best to use the proportions of the hat as a guide.

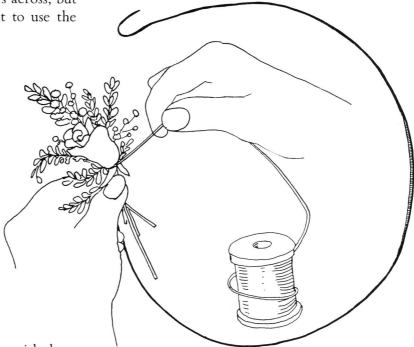

Beginning the floral garland for the hat

■ When you have filled the wire frame with these flowers and reach the end, cut all the stalks and wires as short as possible and bind them securely onto the frame. Cover the wire with a small piece of parafilm. Connect the two hooks together and you will find that the first bunch of the garland will cover the final stems. Through this small space, thread a 1.25 cm (½″) wide piece of ribbon and tie a bow.

■ Place the finished garland on the hat with the ribbon at the back, making sure that you have it straight. Glue the garland into position using the hot glue gun, first the front, then the back and both sides. Each time you put a small amount of glue on the hat, you will need to press and hold the garland in position until the glue has set. Use small flowers and bits of foliage to fill any ugly gaps by gluing them directly onto the garland.

OOSE POSY

REQUIREMENTS
0.55 mm (24 gauge) green floral wire
0.24 mm (32 gauge) green floral wire
Green parafilm
Wire-cutters
Secateurs
1.25 cm (½″) wide deep pink ribbon —
enough for five double-looped bows (for each
bow you will need 53 cm (21″) of ribbon

Foliage:
Maidenhair fern *(Adiantum capillus-veneris)*,
pressed (1)

Line Establishing Flowers:
Lavender *(Lavandula)*, air-dried (2)
Larkspur *(Delphinium ujacis)*, air-dried (3)
Small delphiniums *(D. hybridum)*, air-dried (4)
Blue and white smoke statice *(Limonium perezii*
and *L. tartarica)*, air-dried (5)

Filler Flowers:
Statice *(Limonium)*, air-dried (6)
South Australian daisies *(Ixodia achilleoides)*, air-
dried (7)
Hydrangea *(Saifragaceae)*, air-dried (8)
Strawflowers *(Helichrysum)*, air-dried (9)
Soft white paper daisies *(Leucochrysum albicans)*,
air-dried (10)
Baby's breath *(Gypsophila paniculata)*

Focal Point Flowers:
Roses *(Rosa)* (11)
Small, pale pink, double tulips *(Tulipia)* (12)

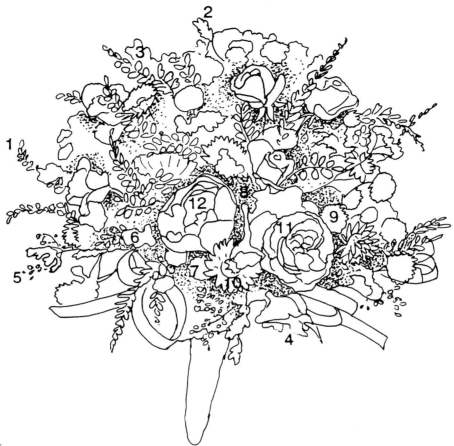

PREPARATION

Prepare the flowers and foliage you intend to use so that they are dried, waxed, glued and sealed as necessary. Note that not all the flowers and foliage will need to be wired for this posy. I usually wire most of the flowers and foliage that make up the outline and the central pieces, as well as a few of the pieces which create the overall shape. Most of the silica-dried Focal Point Flowers will already be wired. Any other material can be added with unwired, natural stalks.

METHOD

- Seven flowers are needed for the outline, which is similar to the outline of the Table Centre Arrangement (page 54). They should all be the same length and include the smallest of every kind of flower that is in the posy. Using the 0.24 (32 gauge) wire, secure the seven false stalks together and bend them at right angles to the stem of the posy.

- Now insert seven pieces of maidenhair fern between the outline flowers, as well as a piece in the centre which should be slightly longer than the outline pieces. The centre flowers should be small and pointed and placed next to this piece of foliage.

- Work from the outline into the centre, gradually building up the density of the flowers to make a good overall shape using the Line Establishing Flowers and the small Filler Flowers.

- Add the Filler Flowers. The larger, shorter flowers should be placed nearer the centre. Try not to work in sections — by continually turning the posy as you work, it will stay balanced. Have flowers with many variations in stem length to give the posy a more natural look. Group the flowers from one side of the posy to the other, merging each group smoothly into the next.

- The Focal Point Flowers can now be inserted. For a small posy, three lovely roses would be suitable, placed at even intervals deep within the posy.

- Use buds and small pieces of wired baby's breath or blue and white smoke statice to lighten the look of the posy, dotting them throughout the centre and around the edge. To finish off, make five double-looped bows and place them evenly around the edge of the posy. Cut the handle to the required length and cover with green parafilm.

STEP-BY-STEP GUIDE TO TWO-LOOPED BOW

This is a four-step process for making the two-looped bows used in the Loose Posy and the Tussie Mussie.

Step 1
Leave one end of the 1.25 cm (½″) wide piece of ribbon hanging down. With the other end, make a loop, followed by a second loop. Keep the loops held firmly between your thumb and forefinger.

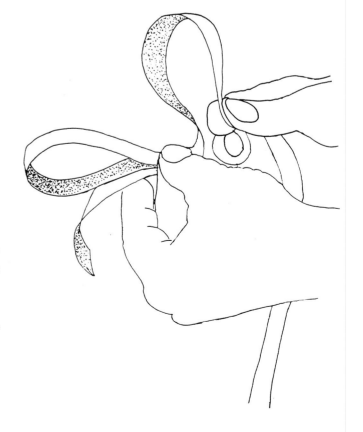

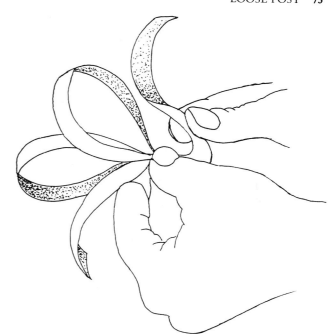

Step 2

Once you have completed the second loop, check that the two ends of the ribbon are a similar length.

Step 3

Hold the looped ribbon firmly between your thumb and forefinger. Place a piece of 0.55 mm (24 gauge) wire at the back of this bow and bend both ends of the wire down to form a hairpin. One end should be much shorter than the other. Wind the longer end around the shorter end and the bottom of the bow two or three times.

Step 4

Cover the wire with green parafilm, using the same technique you would use for a false wire stem.

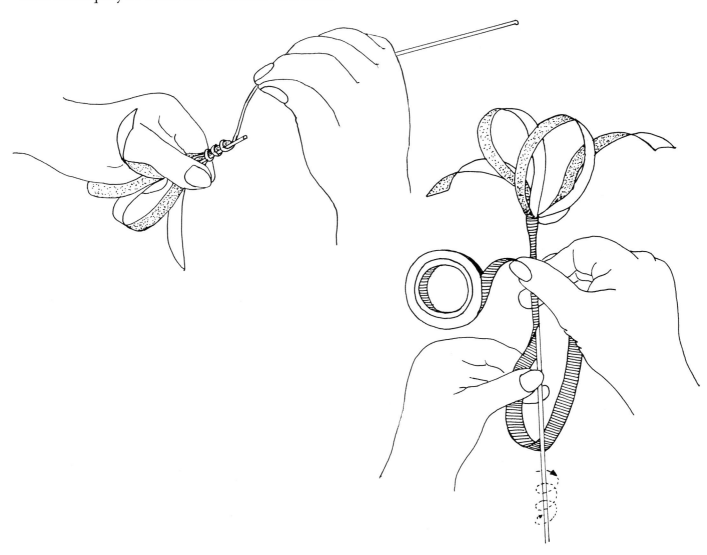

Tussie Mussie

In Elizabethan England, people made little nosegays (small posies) of aromatic herbs and flowers. They carried and sniffed these posies to help disguise the dreadful smell of London streets. These posies often included herbs such as lavender (*Lavandula*), rosemary (*Rosmarinus*) and rue (*Ruta*), which were thought to be disinfectants and to give protection against the plague and other diseases.

During the Victorian era, nosegays became more stylised and were given as tokens of affection. Each herb and flower was chosen to represent a specific message, e.g., rosemary for remembrance, and rosebuds, love. Tussie mussies make wonderful presents and are extremely easy and rewarding to make.

REQUIREMENTS
0.24 mm (32 gauge) green floral binding wire
0.55 mm (24 gauge) green floral wire
Green parafilm
Wire-cutters
Secateurs
1.25 cm (½″) wide ribbon — enough for five double-looped bows
Flower oils

Flowers and Foliage:
Roses *(Rosa)* — one large, well-opened rosebud, three smaller rosebuds, silica-dried (1)
Three strawflowers *(Helichrysum)*, air-dried (2)
Pink pepper berries *(Schinus molle)*, air-dried (3)
Pink larkspur *(Delphinium ujacis)*, air-dried (4)
Lavender *(Lavandula)* (5) and lavender leaves, air-dried
Rosemary *(Rosmarinus)*, air-dried (6)
Blue-green hydrangea *(Saxifragaceae)*, air-dried (7)
Lamb's tongue *(Stachys lanata)*, air-dried (8)
Artemesia *(Anthemis)*, air-dried (9)
Oregano *(Origanum vulgare)*, air-dried
Sage *(Salvia officinalis)*, air-dried

PREPARATION
Ensure that all flowers and foliage have been dried successfully, and that any waxing, wiring, gluing and sealing has been carried out so that they are ready to use.

METHOD
- Begin by surrounding the large rosebud with sprigs of artemisia (a dried grey foliage). Bind the stems together in one place beneath the rose using 0.24 mm (32 gauge) binding wire.

- Add another circle of fragrant herbs, e.g. lavender flowers. I use 'Munstead', which has dainty heads in a lovely deep blue. Single heads can be used on their natural stalks. However, three heads wired together using a 0.55 mm (24 gauge) wire can look even more effective. Again, bind together underneath the central rose.

■ Repeat this process of adding circles of fragrant herbs and flowers, e.g. the three smaller rose buds in one circle and the three strawflowers in another, varying the colours and leaf shapes from row to row, until the tussie mussie is the size that you want. For the last circle, use a large-leaved herb such as sage or lamb's tongue.

■ To give a formal effect, the tussie mussie can be finished off by creating a collar using a paper doily or crepe paper with a frilled edge, held in place with a ribbon. For a more simple or informal look, I finish off with five two-looped bows (pages 74-5) placed evenly behind the edging of sage or lamb's tongue. You can add a few drops of a concentrated flower oil, e.g., lavender, rose or rose geranium, to heighten the aroma of the flowers and herbs you have used.